In the Clo

Jane Hearn
Illustrated by Chi Chung

Rigby®

A Harcourt Achieve Imprint

www.Rigby.com
1-800-531-5015

Mika and her family were going
to see her grandma.
But her grandma lived far away.
So they had to fly on an airplane.
Mika had never been on an airplane before.

Mika and her family sat in their seats.
Mika looked outside and saw there were
lots of clouds in the sky.
They looked big and soft.
Mika wondered how the plane would fly
through the clouds.

4

The pilot came to say hello.
Mika asked, "How does the plane
fly through the clouds?"

The pilot said, "Well, clouds are made up of air and water drops."

"Since clouds are not solid, airplanes can pass right through them."

The pilot went to fly the plane.

The plane made a lot of noise.

It went very fast.

Then it was flying in the air!

Mika saw the clouds get closer.
Then the plane flew right through them!
The clouds looked like cotton.

Soon the plane was above the clouds.

Mika looked up.

She saw a blue sky.

Mika looked down.

She saw white clouds.

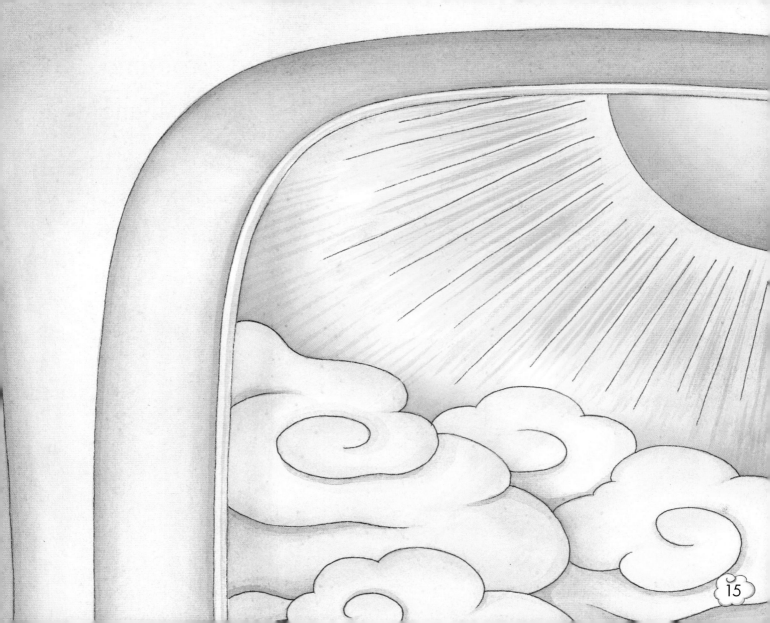

The plane landed, and Mika saw Grandma. Mika could not wait to tell her about flying in the clouds.